Invited to the Feast

BONNIE NARADZAY

Invited to the Feast

poems

SL/\NT
BOOKS

INVITED TO THE FEAST
Poems

Copyright © 2025 Bonnie Naradzay. All rights reserved. Except for brief quotations in critical publications or reviews, no part of this book may be reproduced in any manner without prior written permission from the publisher. Write: Permissions, Slant Books, P.O. Box 60295, Seattle, WA 98160.

Slant Books
P.O. Box 60295
Seattle, WA 98160

www.slantbooks.org

Cataloguing-in-Publication data:

Names: Naradzay, Bonnie.
Title: Invited to the feast: poems / Bonnie Naradzay.
Description: Seattle, WA: Slant Books, 2025
Identifiers: ISBN 978-1-63982-206-5 (hardcover) | ISBN 978-1-63982-205-8 (paperback) | ISBN 978-1-63982-207-2 (ebook)
Subjects: LCSH: Poetry | American Poetry | American poetry 21st century

Contents

I
Paradise in the Day Shelter | 3
Bede's Sparrow | 4
Hymn | 5
Haiku | 6
The Third Person | 7
The Intangible | 8
Lament for a Mentor | 9
Visitation | 10
Elegy with Contrails | 11
The Last Evening | 12
The Piano | 13
A Greek Myth | 14
"Misery" | 15
Meditation (Rain) | 16

II
On the Day of My Birth | 19
O Florida | 20
Summer of Love | 21
Weekend Pass | 22
Bathing in Benares | 23
Picking Blackberries near Bunratty | 24
Dingle Peninsula | 25
Do Not Hurry Your Journey | 26
Presence | 27
Ubi Caritas | 28
Holy Cross Abbey, Early November | 29
Another Sunday in Ordinary Time | 30

Ghazal | 31
Panis Angelicus | 32
Reading Dante | 34
Crows on Bird Walk | 36
Birmingham Diptych | 37
Hanover County Jail, Commonwealth of Virginia | 38
In the Re-Entry Unit, 2a | 39
How To: Broccoli | 40
Shurbaji's Shirt | 41
Now We Are All Sons of Bitches | 42
Reading about Purgatory After Watching Canada Geese Glide Through An Algae-Filled Pond | 43
I Imagine Writing This on a Wall After Drinking Wine | 44
Meditation (Intermission) | 45

III

Personae | 49
A Distant Place | 50
Keys to the Kingdom | 52
Let Me Be | 54
Lazarus | 55
Interpreting Signs | 56
Poem with a Phrase From Bishop | 57
Lines | 58
From Ibykos fragment #286: Why I am Here | 59
    Aporia | 60
    The Night Gardener | 61
    What Is Life? | 62
Sestina: Heraclitus | 63
Gilgamesh at the Retirement Center | 65
Sunday Afternoon on Extended Wings | 66
Sehnsucht | 68
This Present Life | 69
After the Poetry Salon | 70
Meditation (Filling Our Lives) | 71

Notes | 73
Acknowledgements | 76

I

Somebody who is looking out a closed window cannot explain the strange movements of a passer-by. He cannot tell what sort of storm is raging out there or that this person might only be managing with difficulty to stay on his feet.

—*Ludwig Wittgenstein to his sister Hermine*

PARADISE IN THE DAY SHELTER

What they liked best was the poem about a paradise
you can conceal in your pocket so no one will steal it.
Queenie, who stows her hearing aids in a Ziploc bag
in her pocket, asks what free verse is. It's verse that you
don't have to pay for, Chuck tells her. Paul asks if
paradise is a place. Mo shakes his head and says, It's
a sleeping bag at night that can turn into a jacket
in the morning. Leon, who sleeps nearby on the steps
outside St. Paul's, thinks Paradise could be a place
to live: a tent or camper. I say, You would need
a big pocket for that! Saul asks, If I see it, will I
recognize it? Carl says, If you speak of Paradise,
you must consider Hell and the duality of existence.
Well, Jimmy Buffet sang of cheeseburgers in Paradise,
Eugenia replies, and a slice of onion is heaven on earth.

BEDE'S SPARROW

Poems sway like sensate trees; they don't just stand there
stripped of leaves. I have heard Carl, who sleeps

near the M Street Bridge, say he likes how the shadows
of birds' wings pass over his heart. I have seen the robin

lying dead on the sidewalk. Did it fall from the sky,
unlike the geese that glide overhead trailing their legs

in flight, or the starlings appearing to wait in the wings
only to vanish from sight? I have lifted my eyes

to the rafters and seen Bede's sparrow pass through
the church basement and vanish into the dark.

HYMN

Our poetry group—the one I convene in the room behind
the Episcopal Church of the Epiphany at 13th & G—
can hear the organist next door play hymns by Bach

as I explain that a metaphor compares one thing
to another. When I suggest a prompt for next week,
Mo says, "We can't do homework because we're homeless."

Eric, who writes about addiction, laughs delightedly. We all
join him, with Bach chiming in. Later, in the church garden,
I behold a cardinal immersed in a ritual bath, feathers slowly

spreading, wing by wing, while the water sparkles in the sun—
that great ball of fire. Here, as the sky becomes suffused with light,
I miss my son, and I think of the woman whose son died in a fire.

In her grief she spoke to him through a disconnected telephone
on a hill above the sea. "I couldn't hear him, but he heard me,"
she said. "I can go on living now." It's like I'd been there with her.

HAIKU

This morning we read haikus.
Not just Basho, whose name
means "plantain tree," and Issa,
whose name means "cup of tea,"
but also Richard Wright,
born in Mississippi, who later moved
to France and wrote thousands
of haikus in his final years.
When I said Wright followed
the strict syllable count,
Leon asked, "What are syllables?"
I began to count the sounds
on my fingers: *The crow flew so fast /*
that he left his lonely caw.
Two people liked this one by Issa—
Once in the box
every one of them is equal—
the chess pieces.
Eugenia wrote about three women,
regulars here, who died from drugs
in the past few weeks.
"Now in a box," she wrote,
naming each of them in her poem.
Alessandro, responding to Basho,
wrote about constellations of stars.
And for the first time this year
Robert, tattooed up and down his arms,
was awake and sublimely alert.
He liked Issa's *The distant mountains /*
are reflected in the eye / of the dragonfly.
In his eyes I saw myself reflected too,
and over the lonely fields, the crow.

THE THIRD PERSON

For months I visited him weekly, in the mornings—
before pressure built up from fluids as the day progressed.

We shared memories from the poetry sessions we'd led
all those years with the homeless people downtown.

A hospice nurse showed up every week to see
how he was *progressing*, he told me.

When I saw him that last time, he advised me to try
writing poems in the Third Person to distance myself.

"Pretend it happened to someone else."

That last time, his wife chatted about *Madame Bovary*,
which she listened to at night. The awful ending.

After he died, I went away and crossed the Tweed River;
it flows between England and Scotland.

On the first day of fishing season there, I saw a priest bless
the river with whiskey as the salmon swam home.

THE INTANGIBLE

We had pierced the veneer of outside things—
—Ernest Shackleton

He remembered the frozen hours he'd endured
with his two companions as the three crossed over
South Georgia—those icy mountains, the glaciers.

All that time he'd said nothing about the presence
he'd felt had been there—then Worsley spoke
of sensing someone, and Crean confessed to it too.

They shared this while sheltering from the wind
under the lee of a rock, their arms wrapped around
each other for warmth, trying to stay awake.

If someone walks around a bend in the river,
that person has vanished from sight,
like a leaf dropping out of the sky.

But don't I wait to discern if the person
will return—and walk this way? Or look for
the leaf to see where it fell?

Today I discovered the pamphlet of prose poems
you had given me: all I need for now,
as if you had not died after all.

Trying to describe the presence he'd felt, Shackleton quoted
Keats, who wrote about "the dearth of human words,
the roughness of mortal speech."

LAMENT FOR A MENTOR

For Stanley Plumly

Like every other griever, I choose a flower, a violet.
—from "Brownfields"

He said to put myself in the poem,
though I had written about the potato famine.
Have you been to Ireland? he asked.

Yes, to Dingle, I said—on the peninsula
where sheep graze, and the Blaskets,
where seals bob in the shadows

of the tide that will take us away.
He asked if I could film that scene.
Stay in the moment, he said. Be a guide,

for you can't disappear in the poem
or let your mind get lost in memories.
Poetry is meditation and a looking back,

he said. And don't be in a hurry to send out
poems. Let it take years. It's awful when
you can't get what you want.

What matters most is how the pain
can try to weigh you down.
Then you must start all over again—

VISITATION

Henry serves sherry and we talk of the sonnets
of Michelangelo that he's reading now.
I give him a jar of honey from local bees;

we marvel at their lives and how they die,
at season's end, their wings grown thin.
Henry has a broken shoulder; he fell

from the treadmill in the fitness room,
alone, after speeding up, not slowing down.
At 98, he must heal on his own, his arm

immobilized across his chest, hand swollen
and hydrangea blue. Fearing to stay too long,
I leave, though I'd like to cheer him on.

I think of my father, that time I visited him
at the VA hospital in Phoenix, his eyes alert
with pain. I gave him a silk screen painting

of a sailboat gliding over azure and gold,
rising up or sinking below the waves.
I imagine his final trip, anchor weighed,

while I stay ashore, growing smaller,
waving, as high-flying clouds appear
and winds turn his sails into wings.

ELEGY WITH CONTRAILS

To my father

As I hold the phone and strain to hear that you have died,
I look out the window. Cardinals, the birds of winter,

weave among the barren limbs of trees, and contrails
blur in the indifferent sky on Christmas Eve.

Your French wife, with her loaded revolver, hoping
you'd shoot yourself instead, had told me *Don't come*

in September, but I did. *Don't cry,*
she warned me then. *He'll think he's dying.*

Mother, here for the holidays, wears her fringed shawl
with hand-sewn Chinese asters. She lounges on the couch

near the angel-topped tree, frowns when I share the news.
He should have given me more money.

Soon I will prepare a Christmas dinner for people
I hardly know, beans amandine with goblets

of wine, and I will celebrate you. Mother can still
feed herself, act charming, use a finger bowl.

I hold what you gave me for the children:
your pilot's wings, pinned to dried leather; the faded

piano medal wrapped in pale satin; and the watch—
still faintly ticking—from your large, bony wrist.

THE LAST EVENING

After Rilke

As if forgetting where he was,
after coming home from work,
still wearing his military uniform,
he sat ramrod straight at the piano
in the hallway and began to play.

I'd surprised him with sheet music
for *The Well-Tempered Clavier*,
knowing the last time he'd played
was for Rachmaninoff, a competition
in a Chicago concert hall, so long ago.

He must have desired to be alone,
my father, he must have known,
as his fingers searched out the keys,
that everything before his marriage

was wiped away. Would not return.
Mother complained. His desire, gone.
Near his hat, an unfamiliar image:
a figure of death with its head in the stars.

THE PIANO

The ivory keys turned amber at the edges
like the Nutcracker's ludic wooden teeth.
One fluted Doric piano leg

wobbles on its wheel. The well-wrought mahogany
beast is dark with age. The inside pieces,
cracked. It seems the damper action's shot.

Sounds reverberate. The tuner fits the framework
back together. Like a surgeon who sews
a faltering heart, he says it can't

be salvaged again. If Mother were still alive,
I might hear her play *Malagueña*,
several exuberant measures,

or the first few notes of the Moonlight Sonata.
Then she arises from the bench. Flowing
toward the bathroom in a negligee,

she sings a coda in her off-key soprano:
Orchi Chornia—Dark Eyes. A sense of
the tragic. Her repertoire is done.

A GREEK MYTH

Mother wore a nightgown and peignoir, the white filmy kind,
walked barefoot out the front door and into our back yard
to sit in her crescent-moon-shaped rose garden,
her tangled hair caught in the rattan chair.

Those were the days when she got out of bed before noon.

O Étoile de Hollande, her favorite deep red rose—so fragrant.
Did she imagine it could be heaven, where she sat
with her breakfast tray, melba toast, the loose tea leaves
floating in the china teapot?

Much later, when my parents moved again,
there was no rose garden.
On good days, she climbed a stunted apple tree
and set her tray on the low gnarled branch in front of her.

My father pointed to the tree when I came home from college once.

Having come into an inheritance
she spent the cash on trips to Ireland and some Greek islands,
going by herself, never told me, and invested the rest
with hopes of getting rich but the broker swindled her.

Gone, except for this photo she kept of wildflowers in Delos—

She used to sing—*I am weary unto death*—

"MISERY"

When I heard Beethoven's Fifth played on a guitar,
what stood out were the squeaks the fingers made,
like shoes in a basketball game.

My violin teacher puts out food for the birds.
Then he rosins his bow in long strokes before tuning.

At the park, a man was eating mulberries from a tree.
I knew he could not be from here.
The Levant, he said, as we reached for a branch.

You have to reach a certain level of despair,
James Baldwin wrote, to deal with your life at all.

In Chekhov's "Misery," no one wanted to hear the driver
mourn his son, so he talked to his mare in the stable
at night, leaning against her neck.

MEDITATION (RAIN)

A prayer of the people of Athens: "Rain, beloved Zeus,
Rain on the cornfields and the plains of Attica." One
ought to pray thus simply and freely or not pray at all.
—Marcus Aurelius

Rain, inundating, all over, now mixed with snow.
Not long ago, I drove for miles in a torrential storm
to a lecture on Ugolino's tears, and what did I learn?
Now I think of Natasha, who wants to conjure Andrei
from beyond the door of death, so she can talk again
with him, comprehend what he meant back then,
change the outcome. Trying to imagine him, so close—
My father, two days before he died at the VA hospital,
sat up, I was told, one arm outstretched, reaching
towards the silk painting I'd sent: a wall hanging
of a sailboat, floating on waves, within rays of sunlight.
A nurse, finding him motionless there, as in a tableau,
called out to him. From deep within, his voice:
"It would have been a good death." Oh rain, rain—

II

A lively understandable spirit
Once entertained you.
It will come again.
Be still.
Wait.

—Theodore Roethke, "The Lost Son"

ON THE DAY OF MY BIRTH

Dagwood is taking a bath when Mr. Dithers barges in.
Japanese minefields explode in Manila.
Roosevelt, Churchill and Stalin meet at the summer palace
of Czar Nicholas II in Yalta, sign an agreement
to uproot fascism, Nazi-ism, and militarism too.
Dagwood is taking a bath and Mr. Dithers slips on the soap.
Nazi officials remove 100 tons of gold from Berlin and stash it
in a salt mine in Eisenach. My mother asks for ice cream.
The College of William and Mary suspends the student paper
when the editorial urges the admission of Negroes.
The German army in Kharkov imprisoned a Russian soldier,
Ivan, and sent him to Germany to work in an iron foundry,
then on a farm. When the Americans closed in,
the farmer he worked for hid him in the barn, brought Ivan food
for weeks, including tins of pineapple chunks, then disappeared.
Ivan, still hiding, foraged in the orchards at night.
Not knowing the German army had left, he lived inside
a bundle of unthreshed wheat. American soldiers find him
buried there, tell him the Russian army is near Berlin.
Ivan weeps.   My mother asks for ice cream.
   The College of William and Mary.
                    Dagwood takes a bath.

O FLORIDA

Winters were mild. We imported peyote,
practiced missionary acts on rattan mats.
Cockroaches waved their ludic feelers at us.
We faked our IDs.

Mr. Aycock, in Existential Lit,
taught us that free will is just like refusing
painkillers when sitting in the dentist's chair.
It sounded easy.

Real flamingos hung out at the nearby pool,
idly standing on single legs to see us
walk the plank by falling off the diving board
because we felt free.

We scanned verses and crammed marijuana seeds
in Louisiana Picayunes just to
blow smoke rings in the air near our professor,
a sad PhD.

Eels hid in weeds submerged in the placid lake
where we waterskied close to the cypress trees
hung with curlicues of gray-green Spanish moss.
Our own Innisfree.

SUMMER OF LOVE

E detto l'ho perche doler ti debbia
—*Inferno, xxiv, 151*

In our Somerville rental, the brown paper bag
near our kitchen sink was filled with a week's
midden heaps. Sodden garbage rotted on the floor,
and maggots, impersonating rice, writhed free.

Pulverized garlic, which we wore in our socks,
stalked through our nightmares while we slept.
By daylight, strange fumes leapt from our tongues.
Our Siamese cat, in heat, streaked out the door.

Lowell told our King James Bible class he was off
to Brazil, but he only got as far as McLean Hospital,
in Belmont, for a cure. I was the night attendant
who dozed in the hallway, propped against the wall.

Alba, the promising dropout, lit hash on our stove
and sucked up the smoke through a rolled-up fifty.
He stole my Chaucer, Keats, and Bede and sold
them to the used book emporium in Central Square.

Weekends, up in Vermont, we gathered sheaves
of marijuana from the VFW's front yard and dried
the lot in a Laundromat. We sold it all in tie-dyed bags
at steep discounts. Leaves curled like little fists inside.

By summer's end, there was nothing we believed in.
Yams sprouted vines that crawled away
from us, and bancha tea could not keep us awake.
And I have told you this to make you grieve.

WEEKEND PASS

Forsan et haec olim meminisse juvabit.
—The Aeneid

Fresh from electroshock,
now placid and subdued,
the undergraduate plays chess
with an attendant on work-study
from Northeastern U.
The tall robotic kid on Thorazine,
from Dorchester, wears padding
under his shirt to look like Superman.
The forty-ish Art History scholar
with wispy hair overdosed in despair
when her doctor failed to appear.
Now she wants a weekend pass.
The Ivy League dropout
blinks a warning in Morse code
behind her owl-like frames.
Before coming here,
the scholarship student
who made Green Giant costumes
on his sewing machine
slept only two hours a night.
Here, the bedspread prints
chenille designs
on one side of his face.
In the Day Room,
the TV gives off static.
The Quiet Room is entirely white.
Perhaps one day it will help
to remember even this.

BATHING IN BENARES

The sun glints off the backs
of water buffalo that plow
through monsoon paddies in the heat.
At dusk, along the pilgrimage road,
Sanyasi wrapped in saffron
chant their Sanskrit prayers,
hold out their begging bowls for rice.
Death hovers in the ash-strewn air.
Marigold and jasmine garlands
adorn the penitents who flow
in crowds toward *ghats* to soak.
Harijans put sandalwood paste
on their fly-encrusted dead. When
fires lick the high-caste corpse
that floats away on its pyric boat,
flames illuminate the drifting,
fragrant smoke. Whole generations
silt this river. Wade in with me.

PICKING BLACKBERRIES NEAR BUNRATTY

Through stony fields of black-legged sheep,
grazing cows, you walk down a rain-soaked
rutted dirt road narrowed with overgrown
hedgerows: Queen Anne's lace, wild carrot,
morning glories, angelica, blooming thistles,
nettles, dock and sprawling blackberry stalks
with their abundant ripe fruit sucked on by bees
and green-headed flies in the afternoon sun—
berries, dark red and purple on the same drooping
stem, with tough fluted leaves and thorns
that scratch up your hand now straining to reach them
even though your bulging fists smart from nettles
and stickers hiding in thickets rake your arms.
Into the pail go dock leaves to rub out the stinging rash.
Taking the same way back, you discover
ripe berries you missed going out. On this side
of the hedges, higher than your head, you sense
a horse in the next pasture is moving at your pace—
his hushed breath makes you shiver.
These berries will not last; they'll bleed, grow fuzz,
and rot. So you stew them in a pot with chopped green-
skinned apples and burn your tongue devouring
the end of summer, pouring it all into you.

DINGLE PENINSULA

I'm out behind Fran Ryan's, near the hedgerow
    furious with fuchsia and blackberry vines,
searching for clothespins, hanging laundry on the line.

    Marvelous, the way shirts flap and wave their arms
this windy morning as if at the rainbow
    fading from the backdrop of gray skies clearing

to the west. Here above the bay I can see
    Skellig Michael jut up from the Atlantic,
eight miles from land: it's that otherworldly slab

    of rocks where monks, like the Desert Fathers,
sought holy solitude six centuries after Christ.
    Attacked by Vikings, the windblown monks

saved rain, boiled herbs, ate fish, and plundered eggs
    from puffin nests to survive. They chiseled flights
of stairs in stone and built oratories on the highest ledge.

    Oh, let me live always in such ecstatic winds,
about to crash into the sea, where windhovers climb the sky
    and wildly gesturing shirts fly off the line.

DO NOT HURRY YOUR JOURNEY

to the Isola di San Michele,
the Island of the Dead.
As you set out on the *vaporetto*
from Venice, the city swathed
in scaffolding and sinking
into its canals, pass Torcello
with its malarial swamps, poppy fields,
lagoons—and rejoice that you are old
by the time you first behold, from the water,
the high brick walls and dense cypress trees
of the Isola, for it has always lain half-buried
in your mind. When you reach it,
go find the ancient bone heaps entombed
in the Renaissance church, guarded
with carvings of stone angels,
where monks still tend the reliquaries.
But do not hurry the journey at all.
Better if it lasts for years, so you arrive
laden with all you've lost along the way.
Otherwise you could not have expected
such peace among the stacked memorials
guarded by seagulls, lizards, and hooded crows.

After Cavafy

PRESENCE

In the middle of my journey through Cornwall on the Atlantic side,
six hours by train from Paddington, though I was there
during a lonely time in January,
                    I grew to like it without meaning to:
standing at the shore near the wharves, taking ferries
all day, ordering fish and chips—though you could say
a rootless, solitary life can last for just so long.
                    I thought of Ovid,
the poems he sent home after he was banished far to the north
of Rome at a Black Sea outpost, after his urgent pleas to return
went for naught.
              Old man by then, he was reduced to simple gestures
in Tomis, which made *him* the barbarian, not *them*.
                    His Latin verses being worthless now, he began
to enter the language there and realized the people valued friendship,
    as he said in *Tristia*.
            For me, friendship was a small church next to the seawall
on a cold and windy afternoon. Opening the rough-hewn wooden door,
I saw a kindly gentleman standing near the altar;
                  he was sharing his thoughts
about the gifts the Wise Men had brought (it was Epiphany Sunday)
to three old people sitting close to each other on a pew.
      He gestured to me: *Come in, abide with us.*

UBI CARITAS

Winter is piling snow on the porch railings, and ice embraces
      the camellia leaves, the expectant buds. If I forget thee—

I open the door, half expecting the fox to appear,
      trotting down the road in the dark, always going somewhere.

Do the birds go where love is, when evening comes—
      the cardinals, finches, and the others I cannot identify?

When John's disciples start to follow Jesus, he stops to ask—
      what are you looking for? They say—Rabbi, where are you staying?

Come and see, he responds, and they stay with him the rest of the day.
      This was before all the parables and the fish, bread, and wine.

At dawn, between the faint striations of clouds limning the horizon,
      the sun was a transmutation of fire.

Then a flurry of swifts arose—little quarter notes, high in the sky—
      only to disappear, flying into the vanishing point.

The horses have been led out of the stables to graze
      in the dazzling frost-covered grass, the suspension of air.

Maybe the whole world is floating, like the ducks
      where the pond has not yet frozen over. Have mercy on me.

HOLY CROSS ABBEY, EARLY NOVEMBER

The tall, elderly monk who puts out the candles, the last to leave,
pauses and stands blinking before us as if surprised before he turns to go.

In the far pasture where black cows graze, a lone apple tree
still holds its leaves, which are green, not burnished or brown.

Yellow apples, bold neon ornaments, crown the highest branches.
Grass, washed in sunlight, covers the mown fields—

not yet the dull thatch of winter. Is this all a trick of the eye?
Nothing has changed. I have brought my heart to be cracked open

yet I am riveted only by the cows moving single-file down the field
as if they are summoned by an unheard call.

Clouds part to reveal the mountain ridge beyond the Shenandoah.
When I broke the Chinese bowl, my son made it whole.

ANOTHER SUNDAY IN ORDINARY TIME

The pastor walks among us, rolls up his sleeves,
warming to the prophet's teaching this morning—
for Isaiah is preaching we have withered like leaves.

The blind man said he saw men walking like trees,
that time when he was blessed with the gift of seeing.
The pastor walks among us, rolls up his sleeves.

Our guilt is heavy, and our suffering great, reprises
the pastor, while I ponder the miracles of healing
and Isaiah is preaching we have withered like leaves.

It's another Sunday in ordinary time. I look at the frieze
of the Last Supper, the bread, the wine, the final gathering.
The pastor walks among us as he rolls up his sleeves.

On the radio this morning a man said he believes
that people go to church to enter the cloud of unknowing.
Here, Isaiah is preaching we have withered like leaves.

Isaiah wants the brokenhearted to hear his pleas—
his field of vision is like a plow that's still turning.
The pastor walks among us, rolling up his sleeves,
since Isaiah is saying we have withered like leaves.

GHAZAL

With a phrase from Dickinson

At last, the snow. I shoveled the walk before disappearing inside
my black hole; the snow kept on falling anyway.

The hospice worker said the dying regret not having
lived true to themselves before slowly fading away.

Genesis starts over and tells two different creation stories;
we can't even get this right without losing our way.

Earth is close to losing its second moon, and black holes
obliterate galaxies—the stars disappearing, just going away.

Prisoners at Guantanamo, never charged, wrote poems
on Styrofoam cups until guards took even this writing away.

I told my friend I don't think I have a self. He said we all do.
So I tried to say it's somewhere else—not inside hiding, anyway.

White of forgetting, *sustenance of despair*. To find my son, I'd sail
past the pillars of Hercules if I could stop drowning this way.

PANIS ANGELICUS

I saw the finger dripping soot, and felt
the touch, but could not see what others saw
in me. Behind the altar at Holy Rosary,
pastel angels, glowing in halations,
looked at me: a sinner kneeling in their pews.
It's Lent, the place where we left off. Stations
of the Cross, and grief for what's been lost.

I searched for things to do this time to make it
meaningful. Perhaps re-join a choir.
Or ponder ways to make amends to you.
At Madonna House on Capitol Hill,
I learned to decorate *pysanky* eggs
(just empty shells, already hollowed out).
I prayed incessantly that I might hear

from you. Melted beeswax over flames.
Confession? Where to start? I meant to go.
Bewildered by the unfamiliar liturgy
I sang the Mass parts in our choir loft.
Hearing about the Prodigal Son, I thought
of Rembrandt's work, the feast inside the door.
Lent could be perpetual for me,

a chronic state, like being underwater,
suspended, trying not to breathe until
feeling buoyed up when Triduum
arrives, and when I hear from you.
Once more I trudge (no, run—it's late) uphill
to the lay apostolate, passing sentries
on the way, desperate to taste a crumb

of symbolism (hot cross buns) after
chanting psalms in halting antiphons.
At last the dreadful re-enactment came,
rehearsed with incense, accusations:
it descended during fierce winds and snow.
I know a woman who says she has a son
although he fell to his death (with a branch

in his hand) years ago in Rome. About you,
I lie, say "Portland" when friends ask where
you are, and, "He's doing well." Oh, I wasted
Lent, the whole time, spent it like a prodigal,
my loss too great to be absorbed, distracted by
the off-key choir's strangely jarring tunes,
translations that confused me. The empty tomb.

READING DANTE

Unable to discern my way through the darkest woods
(how do you even *know* you're lost), lured by ancient
travelers, I'm reading *The Inferno,* imagining Virgil

at my side. I knit my brows the way old tailors do
when bending over threaded needles in the gloom
and read this marked-up copy, my daughter's text

from high school days, gleaning what she underlined.
I find her penciled comment—"the journey's
universal." Later she writes, "What you don't see

is often more important than what you see."
And then I see Ulysses in the flames and read
where Virgil intercedes, telling Dante not to speak,

since Homer's Odysseus speaks classical Greek.
Why does his restless search enthrall me so? Ovid,
himself an exile, seized on what Tiresias foretold,

while Dante continued the story where Ovid ceased,
after Ulysses set out to sea. Who guides a pilgrim
to the good, and what's the way to virtue and wisdom?

Ulysses heads for the sun as it sinks in the west. I still
mourn his ending. In Auschwitz, Primo Levi speaks
to his friend Pikolo about *The Inferno* and struggles to recall

the lines he learned in school—Ulysses' finest speech—
when the aging king exhorts his men to take the oars again.
"Listen," says Levi, in a terrible hurry to deliver the soup

—cabbage and turnips—that day. Feeling the sea close
over his head, Levi reaches the Pillars of Wisdom and quotes,
For you were not formed to live the life of brutes.

CROWS ON BIRD WALK

Mark holds up his bird-call impersonator
    then says he is telling the wood peewee we are friends
        but to me it might as well be Church Slavonic

a crow after flying away leaves its caw behind
    the tails of barn swallows fork but the crow's tail does not
        we may have seen two eastern meadowlarks

one bird with a distinctive cry is saying lookatme lookatme
    John Wilkes Booth's last words were useless useless
        wrens sound as if they're scolding us

the Carolina Wren says teakettle teakettle
    why do birds risk their lives to sing
        a starling pecks at horse manure a flycatcher works the till

I tell Bob about the bird trapped in the Nashville airport
    he puts a sprig of invasive stilt grass in his bird notebook
        between its lines like crows' feet

purple martins soar above the baseball field
    someone points to a crow walking along the road
        that bows its head at every step as if to genuflect

BIRMINGHAM DIPTYCH

After Dawoud Bey's "Birmingham Project"

involuntarily I am pulled back   to that September morning
to Sunday the blue skies that day   the moment before,
the moment after   what would it be like
to resurrect those   who never went on to have a full life
under this silent sky,   tall branching trees
but the past will not come back   I had to embrace them
this is a classroom, the lunch counter   the back of his neck, the barber shop
quiet blue skies riding by   as if a child is looking out the car window
the trees the lost feeling of holiness   and underneath,
the seething   the split screen
the lampposts, the tops of buildings   then the classroom appears,
with crayon drawings   about not giving up
eyes focused   they are looking through shattered glass
not blurred but clear   as the journey ends
                                      the church comes into view

HANOVER COUNTY JAIL, COMMONWEALTH OF VIRGINIA

Lunch today for the inmates means white bread
and a slice of baloney. Dinner is more of the same.
The limit now—two meals a day to stay in budget.
The jail's run by a profit-making corporation.
Vending machines hold other selections,
like undated Twinkies and cinnamon buns.
Immigration rents beds here
for young, married Chinese women
without papers, only fake passports they bought in haste.
Fearing reprisals, they fled the provinces, their homes and families.
For one bore a child after marrying too young, at twenty,
and another had a second child, a girl.
One has an abscessed tooth.
I write down her plight,
mainly that she cannot pay a Chinese-speaking lawyer
in New York City, her only hope, or even call long distance,
collect. I scan the confession, read her gestures.
The budget does not fund dental work, I'm told.
What's more, they charge for aspirin.
The next one, wearing the same ink-blue pajamas
and plastic shower shoes,
holds her stomach, speaks of constant pain.
The doctor comes once a month
and sees only those who signed up long before.
The system weeds out malingerers, the female warden says,
handing me a sheaf of small-print regulations.

IN THE RE-ENTRY UNIT, 2A

Today I have brought haikus. We count syllables.
        One woman says she writes poems in her head.

Another writes letters to her mother, who died last year.
        Veronica says she's in for drunk driving again

but doesn't belong here. Wanda says her friend
        got four years for DWI after her car rammed

another car, and the other driver wasn't even hurt.
        We read the Basho poem about the frog jumping

into the pond. "What do you see," I ask. The new arrival,
        who wears socks on her arms

because the cellblock is so cold, says it reminds her
        of a dream she had last night,

but the pond in her dream was a lake, muddy and deep,
        with catfish that did not move.

HOW TO: BROCCOLI

This morning we loaded cardboard boxes of vegetables
into the trunks of cars. In each box, we stuck a card:
How to: Broccoli, in tiny print, one side in Spanish.
Families stayed in their cars in July's fierce heat.
To receive the USDA box, they'd filled out a form:
name, address, number of people in each family.
The rule: one box per family, no matter how many,
for a box of surplus white mushrooms, broccoli,
iceberg lettuce, turnips, and fruit. The boxes sagged.
(In church we prayed for the virus to just go away.)
How to eat broccoli raw with a dip, stir fry, or steam.
But there are seven in our family, one man pleaded.
We gave him an extra box. A boy waved at me
from the back seat. One woman said, "We are illegal.
We don't want to put our names down on anything."
(In church we now regard the virus as a wake-up call.)
I put a box in her old car; it shook, about to break down.
(The Pharisees insisted on handwashing, we were told).
Camus said we are owls blinded by too much light.

SHURBAJI'S SHIRT

In a Syrian Prison, from the testimony of Mansour Omari

When they called my name, I grabbed Shurbaji's shirt,
blue and white striped, that he was protecting
for his wedding—as soon as he could get out—
but he gave us his shirt to preserve our names.
The tailor honed a chicken bone for a quill.
Shurbaji, the other journalist there, skilled
at handwriting, etched each of our names on strips
of cloth. We made ink from rust scratched off cell bars,
mixed with blood that Omar slowly collected.
Making the quill a needle now, the tailor
pulled the threads in Shurbaji's shirt to embed
the strips of names inside the cuffs and collar.
Replaced the threads. Omar the tailor is dead.
The first one to leave takes the shirt. When I heard
my name, I grabbed the shirt. They transferred me to
more prisons, still underground. I saved the shirt.
Sweat blurred some names by the time I was set free.
My love, we are coming back. Don't forget us.
Our group of five shared a space of three floor tiles.
Still unfolding in the news: the dead, the names
of us. Eighty-five men sharing lives in there.
She learned that Shurbaji died after three years
in prison. The terrible beatings. *My love,*
My love, we are coming back, Shurbaji sang.
Don't forget us. All our names. My wedding shirt.

NOW WE ARE ALL SONS OF BITCHES

The part about airmen roving through tomato fields in Spain
just before tourist season, hunting for unexploded hydrogen bombs?
I took the whole thing out. Too real, I thought. It actually happened,
like the dying Chernobyl worker, how pieces of his liver, lungs,
his insides, were all sliding from his mouth, his tongue
falling out, his overtime paid in bottles of vodka, touted
to cure the strange sickness. True, but who would believe it?
When the East Germans refused to work without safety garb,
the tone seemed off. I left it in but crossed out the bourgeois
vignette about the peanuts in the silver inlaid dish and, yes,
Brecht's view of the birds from his hospital window in Berlin.
They had to go, and the scholarly quotes, the paraphrased lines,
like "Simonides was a rotten skinflint," for which I substituted
the original Greek: "We are all sons of bitches now."

READING ABOUT PURGATORY AFTER WATCHING CANADA GEESE GLIDE THROUGH AN ALGAE-FILLED POND

Swept in by October's clean blue winds,
the airborne birds deploy their landing gear:
splayed feet like water skis.
They transform their shapes
with nonchalance,
create momentary wakes.
The green slick parts ways.
These are not Mary Oliver's wild geese,
but tell me about despair
and the vestibule of Purgatory
that we're in,
and I will tell you how to let it all go
leaving nothing but a slick green residue of sin.

I IMAGINE WRITING THIS ON A WALL AFTER DRINKING WINE

half-moon floating in the autumn sky
even though it's still afternoon
I sweep the piles of cast-off leaves
from the deck out back
then pause to watch more swirl down
from the tree above
as a squirrel aims another beech nut shell
and familiar music reaches me
from far away
one line and then another
suspended there
yes I know that minuet from Bach
played it years ago
I wait to hear more notes waft through the air
may no leaf fall
at a time like this
as clouds drift by

MEDITATION (INTERMISSION)

. . . what if the master of the show who engaged an actor
were to dismiss him from the stage? "But I have not spoken
my five acts, only three." "What you say is true, but in life
three acts are the whole play."
—Marcus Aurelius

It's all I think about these days, when intermission is,
will it ever come, has it passed, and how many scenes
are in this act that's so interminable, if it's not the last.
Could this be the whole play? Hamlet wanted more time.
The end seems hurried; everyone but Horatio falls dead
at the banquet, then Fortinbras appears. The play's
the thing! Mother's things are boxed up in a pre-fab shed
behind my sister's place. Closets bulge with our belongings,
and what are they for? My father's French wife got rid
of all he owned as soon as he died although I'd wanted
something to remember him by. She had him cremated;
then the VA sent his ashes east to Arlington Cemetery.
My sister wanted a ceremony right away to lay him
to rest behind a small locked door. I could not face it.

III

Sometimes a man stands up during supper
and walks outdoors, and keeps on walking,
because of a church that stands somewhere in the East.
—Rilke, *The Book of Hours, II,19*

PERSONAE

Today we read "Gin River," a poem by Tyree Daye.
In it, Bill Broonzy is singing "When I Been Drinking,"
and people dance in the river, down in rural Carolina.

We end with James Wright's persona poem, "Saint Judas."
When it's time to write, Ibrahim, in the voice of Moses,
dares the Pharaoh to make the sun go from west to east.

Chuck wears the chef's jacket he found in a bag of donations.
On the pocket, stitched in blue cursive: "Ramon."
It's his *nom de plume*. Oh, Ramon—where are you now?

A DISTANT PLACE

With a line from Emily Dickinson

Summer just wants to hoodwink us,
Would slip away from our embrace—

Ensuring we will scarce take note
When she departs with awful grace.

For she would lapse in small degrees
Like slowly disappearing waves

That lap upon the farther shore.
Beguiled by Summer's languid pace,

We're mesmerized by fireflies.
Distracted by the sudden grace

Of a late-blooming rose, we mourn
The muted colors, ravaged face.

Summer then might lengthen twilight,
Confuse us with unwelcome clouds—

While dusk, unseemly in its haste,
Intrudes to make its meaning clear.

Nostalgia will not save us now.
Observe the birds. With folded wings

They start to sing, then steal away
As imperceptibly as grief.

Summer has left us standing here,
Sends postcards from a distant place.

KEYS TO THE KINGDOM

To my mother

We'll never know if the plaques
made a mush of your brain
before you could locate the key

to your dream kingdom.
I wish I could find you there.
Though the death certificate said

that you died of a *bed sore*,
there was more to it
when you lay mute and still

whether awake, eyes dark
like obsidian, or faking sleep,
desperate to get out.

Years before, we did play
tennis, but you rarely
spoke to me. "Good stroke,"

I told myself, since you did not.
It was no use. Speech was a skill
I failed at too—not just with you—

though once as a child I asked
where you and Dad would live
once he stopped flying planes

and ended his Air Force days.
"A Castle in Spain," you said

but did not elaborate.

Instead, he left for good,
only to slowly decompose
from *adenocarcinoma pancreas,*

his mind wholly intact.
Later, you lived with me.
That was when I learned

you'd try to wander off
at sundown. To keep you in,
my sister gave me a bolt

for the front door, and a key,
as if it was that easy.
You were still walking then,

though mute. Found a way out.
A policeman drove you home
after I reported you Missing.

Alighting from his squad car,
you looked like Blanche DuBois,
having seen a different world

kinder than this one.

LET ME BE

After Caravaggio's *The Raising of Lazarus*

If we juggle the stiffened corpse like this,
who knows what harm we'll cause? His arms

splay like branches of a withered olive tree.
What fool's errand is it that we, mourning

Lazarus, are pretending he's simply asleep?
There we are in the painting, looking back

at the weeping rabbi in wild disbelief.
Four days Lazarus lay here, unmoving.

Where are the signs he'll return to this side
of life? His eyes—almost opaque, as if

clouded over. Is he not distraught to leave
the tomb? Even upwind, he stinks. His skin,

like dried petals. He'll not trust unsure feet
to stand. Clumsy legs. Tongue that stumbles

over speech: thin whirring sounds, like locusts
in the wind. He's already started his journey,

swaddled in strips now coming undone.
Let me be, he'll say, and try to climb back in.

LAZARUS

After four days of being elsewhere,
in stillness, maybe asleep, he heard

a voice, sounds of weeping. Disbelief.
Winding cloths began unraveling.

As he rose, then walked unsteadily,
he grew hungry and asked for manna;

Martha cooked barley, which was easy
to get down. He did not ask for more,

wasn't used to small talk, and his eyes
appeared unfocused, looking inward.

We took to following after him. Then
authorities wanted him dead again.

INTERPRETING SIGNS

For my daughter

Born into air,
unpredictable sprite,
she spilled into my life
without slowing down.
It was always like this.

Teaching her to ride
a pink bicycle that June
on Assateague,
I ran alongside,
shouted "I'm holding on,"

as she pedaled faster,
sped up, looked back and laughed,
while keeping her balance,
to see me shrink
behind on the wildlife loop.

Feeling small, I wobbled
back into my own life,
casting a long shadow,
and it wasn't yet noon.

The herons in the wetlands
didn't look up, even
when she rounded the bend,
braked at my feet, and asked
why I let go so soon.

POEM WITH A PHRASE FROM BISHOP

sometimes my sister will e-mail me at 1 a.m.
to say she's feeling distraught and then
at 3 a.m. a message to report she's feeling
so much better now but I don't know this
till I wake the next morning and piece
the sequence together what I mean to say
is she made up her mind again to run away
from her husband in her late-model car
everything was packed but she decided
to stop before setting off at Cuppa Cheer
and pick up the cookies she'd ordered there
she told the nice lady about needing to flee
then the lady who had troubles of her own
said let's pray and wrapped a prayer shawl
around her in a big hug my sister took it
as a sign to stay after all and drove home
just in time to unload before her husband
returned from work the cookies were good
our lives can be like that—*awful but cheerful*

LINES

This has been done before, standing in line for a long time.
Think of Soviet women who queued for hours for bread.
And I have learned about the lines of the Great Depression:
men lined up for mind-numbing jobs at assembly lines.

Think of Soviet women who stood for hours for bread
or Akhmatova outside the prison waiting for news of her son.
Here, men lined up for mind-numbing jobs at assembly lines.
These days some have it easy—food deliveries, yoga online.

Akhmatova outside the prison waited with women for news
and the chance to send a loaf of bread, or a note, inside.
These days some have it easy—food deliveries, yoga online.
Still, Camus said the plague is within us, here to stay.

I have learned about the lines of the Great Depression
where hope envisions a loaf of bread, a note from inside.
Camus wrote that the plague is within us, here to stay,
as it has always done: waiting in line for a long time.

WHY I AM HERE

Using "on the one hand, on the other hand, nay rather" from Ibykos fragment 286 and adding phrases only from Martin Luther King's Letter from the Birmingham City Jail

In Birmingham, on the one hand,
early Christians,
being willing to face hungry lions
where a higher law was involved,
while white mothers
screaming
on television
were seen.
On the other hand, for me
an unjust law distorts the soul.
Nay rather,
like a code
inflicted on a minority,
creating with unjust methods
parading without a permit,
on its face,
nothing
wrong
man's tragic separation.

APORIA

Using "on the one hand, on the other hand, nay rather" from Ibykos fragment 286 and adding phrases only from Plato's Meno

The torpedo fish?
Anyone who touches it feels numb,
on the one hand,
and I am quite perplexed.
On the other hand, the human soul is immortal:
at times it comes to an end, which they call dying,
at times it is reborn, but it is never destroyed,
and one must live one's life
piously.
Nay rather,
the statues of Daedalus run away if not tied down.
But now the time has come for me to go.

THE NIGHT GARDENER

Using "on the one hand, on the other hand, nay rather" from Ibykos fragment 286: and adding phrases only from Benjamin Labatut's When We Cease to Understand the World *(Part IV)*

The night gardener speaks of mathematics,
on the one hand, as former alcoholics speak
of booze, with a mixture of fear and longing,
although he could have lived like a monk,
holed up in the Pyrenees,
while on the other hand,
sometimes he leaves
buckets of compost
outside my house as a gift.
Nay rather,
he wonders if my lemon tree will die
of overabundance,
but says there is no way to know
without cutting it down
and looking inside its trunk.
Who would want to do that?

WHAT IS LIFE?

Using "on the one hand, on the other hand, nay rather" from Ibykos fragment 286 and adding only phrases from the epilogue of Schrödinger's What is Life?

To say "Hence I am God Almighty,"
on the one hand,
sounds both blasphemous and lunatic,
the closest a biologist can get
to proving God and immortality at one stroke.
On the other hand, in the *Upanishads*,
Atman equals Brahman
in perfect harmony, mystics
somewhat like the particles
in an ideal gas.
Nay rather,
in a gallery of mirrors,
like the way Gaurishankar and Mount Everest
are the same peak seen from different valleys,
I see my tree
you see yours
obviously only one tree.
What the tree in itself is,
we do not know.

SESTINA

(UPON READING HEIDEGGER'S ESSAY ON FRAGMENT B50 OF HERACLITUS)

Hippolytus of Rome's the only source
of this figment by the Pre-Socratic otherwise
Called Heraclitus the Obscure, here revealed
To us by Heidegger, from ancient Greek.
He tries to unconceal the thoughts and words
Hiding in the Logos concept that all is One.

Our guide shows how the trackless paths are One
By trekking through the Schwartzwald for the Source:
A clearing from which springs the age-old Word.
Does truth unmask the way to vatic wisdom
When we explore such mysteries in the Greek?
Embody Heraclitus; this too he may reveal.

Dogs bark at strange philosophers who reveal
Confusion by their questioning every one
Of these fragments, arrows from archaic Greek.
Unclothe the cryptic sayings at their source.
If nature hides, why would truth do otherwise?
Accept no hyphenated made-up words.

Step onto the water-logged esoteric words
In Heraclitus's familiar river to reveal
The Wanderer and his shadow. We're none the wiser
Despite knowing that *panta* is all and *ev* is One.
When reason neglects to excavate the Source,
We lose the lit-up filaments of that Greek.

Letting-lie-together-before is *legein* in Greek;
Or could it be "to say, or speak," in other words,

The same, not the same, depending on the source?
Still, our layered readings may reveal
Lyric-like fragments, directed at the One
Divinity of God, where all is wise.

"Within this meaning to say One is All is Wise
When you listen not to me, but to it" (in Greek).
This translation's not the only one,
Yet Heidegger must interrogate these words
To seek the middle voice that will reveal
Heraclitus' mediated source.

One brief light shines on inscrutable words
Missed, otherwise, when we parse the Greek
And plead with Hippolytus to reveal his source.

GILGAMESH AT THE RETIREMENT CENTER

We conclude the annual poetry reading ritual for the residents,
and I delight in the bacon-wrapped scallops impaled on toothpicks.
Ecstatic to find two kinds of wine, I am feeling satisfied.

At some point during dinner, we talk about what we're reading.
When I say I'm enjoying the epic of *Gilgamesh,* Julia asks me
what that ancient tale is all about. I launch into the highlights,

including the grand Sumerian city of Uruk, its meaningful bricks,
the faithful friend Enkido, his tragic death, the subsequent quest
for immortality, how Gilgamesh fails his test by falling asleep

instead of staying awake for a week and loses out on eternal life
(falling asleep again?) when a snake eats the plant and sheds its skin.
Despite all this, Julia thinks I mean the Hindu elephant god, Ganesh.

For a moment I forget who I am, and where. Then I think of Odysseus,
asleep in the boat to Ithaka; Athena disguised the island with mist.
So I change the subject to Odysseus, that time he rises out of the sea

from his exhausting swim, still clutching the rock Calypso gave to him,
and he sees in the rock a mist that parts to show the years ahead. His bed.
The wine is wearing off, so I'll go home and fall asleep like Gilgamesh.

SUNDAY AFTERNOON ON EXTENDED WINGS

We are gathered at Don Pollo's
to read aloud our latest poems,
with Pam stating that hers, in case
we missed it, is on sexual
awakening. Digging into
spit-roasted chicken wings,
we mention ex-husbands.
Norma will like hers more
after he dies. This reminds me
to outlive mine so he won't get
my pension. A Moroccan soccer
player on the big TV whips
off his wild shirt after he scores.
Staring, transfixed, at his rippling
chest and abdomen, I fumble
for words to explain how seeing
his bared body affects me, while
Linda, having already talked
of her new decisiveness in
the garden, now that she's sixty,
her freedom to uproot plants if
they don't fit in, says *it's on all
the talk shows; it's what women want,*
so now I wonder what *it* is
and remember that guy at Squaw
Valley who talked of tantric bliss.
When I was younger, I tell them,
while eating bread pudding from a
Styrofoam plate, *it was always
the high-minded renaissance man
who caught my attention. What a
disaster!* Once more, I glance up

at the soccer game. Do I see
Apollo's torso—his smiling hips
and thighs—or the nameless oarsmen
who rowed Odysseus to shore?

SEHNSUCHT

After Rilke (The Book of Hours, II, 19)

To rise up from dinner,
leave the dishes on the table,
walk out the door, head east,
and go on walking.
I could do that today, leave
my coat behind—the coat
of old mythologies,
feathers flying from the seams—
now that winter is on the way out.
I could do that today in the hush
of the afternoon
as the weather turns undeniably
warm, the air expansive now—
a diaphanous mantle, in subtle colors.
It feels like Vermeer's view of Delft,
the yellow patch of wall, death—
I could go looking for it now.

THIS PRESENT LIFE

Sensus, non ordo
—Bede

How does this present life compare with the time
given to us, on either end? We cannot always

go on singing in the mead hall filled with friends,
passing the flagon and harp around, all while

a cowherd is off having visions in his sleep.
The wind moans outside in dark cathedrals

of black spruce, junipers, and animal sounds.
Is that our afterlife? When a sparrow flies,

as Bede tells it, through a crack in the roof
to the light inside, then out the other way,

he returns to the crying winds and the gloom.
Soon enough, the cold will enter the hall

to kill the warmth with permafrost. Why not
tell the Kentish King instead about the Lord

of Life, who wrote with his finger on the ground
until the Pharisees were gone? What did he write?

That's what I wonder.
This is the sense, but not the words in order.

AFTER THE POETRY SALON

It's time to rise and go, before the doors are closed.
    When I ask what they'd like to read next time,
Tony, who sleeps on the steps of St. Paul's and quotes
    the Psalms, wants more from Yeats. After reading
"The Coat" today, he asked why Yeats would turn away
    from mythologies, if they kept him warm.
Small passing facts: Carl sleeps near the M Street Bridge
    unless the weather's really bad. He likes
Eliot, especially that one about Prufrock.
    Tarik hides clothes near the library. Loves Rumi.
Robert, slowly rising from the table, wants poems
    about the arrival of spring despite
the snow that fell last night and froze the daffodils.
    Last week, after we read poems by Franz Wright,
Sheila wrote about walking to Martha's Vineyard
    when the tide was low. She asks for love poems,
like "How Do I Love Thee," which she once knew by heart.
    Leaning on his cane, Mo says poetry
makes him forget about his troubles and his pain.
    We are nearing the threshold of both worlds.

MEDITATION (FILLING OUR LIVES)

Do not wander from your path any longer, for you are not
likely to read your notebooks or your deeds of ancient Rome
and Greece or your extracts from their writings, which you
had laid up against old age.
—Marcus Aurelius

The future comes in the guise of spring rising all around
after the rain ends and you've planted bulbs into the ground.

Toss out last year's odds and ends. The life you dreamed about
is here. Think of veering completely off the rails or going out

another way, like those disciples on the way to Emmaus,
because you will meet a stranger on your journey, as they must,

and invite the stranger to a feast, which is where you need to be.
Aurelius died near the Danube, far from Rome, and here you are,

perplexed by how to part with rooms full of possessions, notebooks.
Jesus beckons to a tax collector to come with him. Matthew looks

surprised, points to himself and asks, "Who, me?" Then he rises,
goes with him to the banquet. When we are empty, we fill our lives.

Notes

"Paradise in the Day Shelter": the poem that everyone liked was "A Portable Paradise," by Roger Robinson. It is the title poem for his book, *A Portable Paradise*, which won the T.S. Eliot Prize in 2019.

"The Intangible": the title and the quote from Keats come from this section of Shackleton's *South*:

> [In] the unnamed mountains and glaciers of South Georgia, it seemed to me often that we were four, not three. I said nothing to my companions on the point, but afterwards Worsley said to me, "Boss, I had a curious feeling on the march that there was another person with us." Crean confessed to the same idea. One feels "the dearth of human words, the roughness of mortal speech" in trying to describe things intangible, but a record of our journeys would be incomplete without a reference to a subject very near to our hearts.

For the three poems with epitaphs from Marcus Aurelius, I used the translation by A.S.L. Farquharson of the *Meditations*.

"Meditation (Rain)": the quote starting "A prayer of the people of Athens" is from Meditation V.7.

"Meditation (Intermission)": the quote starting "But I have not spoken my five acts, only three" is from the final Meditation, XII.36.

"Meditation: Filling Our Lives": the quote starting "Do not wander from your path any longer" is from Meditation III.14.

Everything in "On the Day of my Birth" came from a newspaper published on that day (though my older sister told me later about my mother asking for ice cream).

"Reading Dante" refers to a section from Primo Levi's *Survival at Auschwitz*, where he quotes a line from Canto 26 of Dante's *Inferno*.

"Now We Are All Sons of Bitches" is what Kenneth Bainbridge, an American physicist, said to Oppenheimer after they oversaw the detonation of the Trinity nuclear device at Los Alamos on July 16, 1945. "Simonides was a rotten skinflint" is a translation from the Greek (from Anne Carson's book, *Economy of the Unlost*). The information about Chernobyl came from *Voices from Chernobyl: An Oral History of a Nuclear Disaster* by Svetlana Alexievich. The poem starts with an incident in 1966, when an American B-52 bomber crashed in mid-air over Spain near Palomares, releasing four unexploded hydrogen bombs. Two fell into the sea. The Air Force immediately deployed low-ranking troops to search for fragments in Spanish fields after the Plutonium-filled detonators of the other two bombs went off on land, spreading three kilograms of highly radioactive Plutonium-239 on the ground.

"Shurbaji's Shirt" is based on the account of Mansour al-Omari, a survivor of a Syrian prison who smuggled out the names of eighty-five prisoners. Shurbaji himself, a journalist, after three years in the prison, died of continued beatings by the guards.

About the Ibykos fragment 286, Anne Carson's translation, and *Nay Rather*: Anne Carson translated this fragment from Ibykos, an ancient Greek lyric poet, and then proceeded to use the structure of the fragment (on the one hand / on the other hand / nay, rather) to experiment with other texts, including pages from Kafka, the FBI file on Bertholt Brecht, and two pages from the owner's manual for her new microwave. See her chapbook, *Nay Rather*. Using four different sources, I followed the structure of the Ibykos fragment that she translated.

"Sehnsucht" refers to Rilke's poem in *The Book of Hours* (Robert Bly's translation):

> Sometimes a man stands up during supper
>   and walks outdoors, and keeps on walking,

because of a church that stands somewhere in the East.
And his children say blessings on him as if he were dead.
And another man, who remains inside his own house,
dies there, inside the dishes and in the glasses,
so that his children have to go far out into the world
toward that same church, which he forgot.

The "yellow patch of wall" in "*Sehnsucht*" (which means "yearning" or "longing" in German) refers to a passage in Proust's *The Captive*: Bergotte, an author, rises from his deathbed to see Vermeer's painting once more and looks for that yellow patch of wall. Shortly afterwards, Bergotte dies. The Polish artist and military officer, Józef Czapski, in a Soviet hard-labor camp, where he and other Polish officers were imprisoned during World War II, presented a series of evening lectures to the others on Proust and how art gives meaning to life. He focused on this passage from Proust about Bergotte in one of his lectures (*Lost Time: Lectures on Proust in a Soviet Prison Camp*, by Józef Czapski).

In "This Present Life," the last line, which is italicized, comes from Bede's comment (in Latin) on his translation of Caedmon's Hymn: "This is the general sense but not the exact order of the words" that he sang in his sleep; for it is impossible to make a literal translation, no matter how well-written, of poetry into another language without losing some of the beauty and dignity." The epigraph for my poem, "*Sensus, non ordo,*" is a shorthand version of the first part of Bede's comment. In "Bede's Sparrow" as well as in this poem, the reference is to Bede's description of the sparrow's brief flight through the rafters—to explain to a pagan king why he might consider conversion to Christianity.

"Meditation (Filling Our Lives)": I had in mind Caravaggio's painting, "The Calling of St. Matthew," completed in 1600 for the San Luigi dei Francesi Church in Rome. Jesus is calling to Matthew to follow him, and Matthew, half rising, illumined by light, points to himself in baffled disbelief, according to one interpretation. (Afterwards, Matthew invites Jesus to a feast.)

Acknowledgements

My deep thanks to all my mentors, including D. Nurkse, David Baker, Stanley Plumly, Michael Collier, David Keplinger, and too many others to name, and to my dear friends over the years in this art, and to the Street Sense and Miriam's Kitchen poetry groups, and the poets at the Ingleside Independent Retirement Community, and to my family. And my gratitude to Gregory Wolfe of Slant Books, who brought this volume into being.

Thanks to the publications in which these poems first appeared:

Agni, American Journal of Poetry, Amethyst Review, Anderbo.com, Anglican Theological Review, Atlanta Review, Birmingham Poetry Review, Cider Press Review, Colloquy, Crab Creek Review, Cumberland River Review, Dappled Things, Delmarva Review, Ekphrastic Review, Epoch, Florida Review Online, Galway Review, Georgia Review, Innisfree, Kenyon Review Online, New Letters, New Verse News, Northern Virginia Review, One, One Art, Passager, Pinch, Poet Lore, Poetry Miscellany, Potomac Review, Rhino, Seminary Ridge Review, Slab, Split This Rock, Tar River Review, Xavier Review.

This book was set in Centaur, designed by the American typographer and book designer, Bruce Rogers, who was commissioned to create an exclusive type for the Metropolitan Museum of Art (New York) in 1914. Based on the Renaissance-period printing of Nicolas Jenson around 1470, it was named Centaur after the title of the first book designed by Rogers using the type: *The Centaur* by Maurice de Guérin, published in 1915. Lanston Monotype of London cut the commercial version of Centaur and released it in 1929.

This book was designed by Shannon Carter, Ian Creeger, and Gregory Wolfe. It was published in hardcover, paperback, and electronic formats by Slant Books, Seattle, Washington.

Cover: Giotto, *The Wedding at Cana*, circa 1305. Arena Chapel, Padua.

www.ingramcontent.com/pod-product-compliance
Lightning Source LLC
Chambersburg PA
CBHW020332090426
42735CB00009B/1510